Table of Contents

FIRST THINGS FIRST

If you read my other books, you know that I fuckin hate wasting somebody else's time. Partly because I don't want you to waste my time either.

If you will not take action, then just refund your purchase and go buy some " get rich quick" course that clearly doesn't work.

If you're one of the few who would rather TAKE ACTION than read, then I got good news for you.

This book will be step by step and will be as concise as possible.

I write this book in a way that even my 12 yr. old brother can implement even if he's not some kind of genius.

The steps will be divided into 4 parts.

1 - Keyword Research

Find keyword "gift ideas" that people are already searching for.

2 - Create a Website

Create a website where they will see these gifts

3 - Write a Product Review

Write a product review of these gifts and sell it to them

4 – Ranking Your Website

Rank your website so someone can actually see it

That's it!

No need to be some kind of ninja internet marketer.

Just plain old smart keyword research and some basic seo stuff. Let's do it!

1 – Keyword Research

This is so simple that you'll laugh why you haven't thought about it.

Simple go to Google's keyword planner

https://adwords.google.com/ko/KeywordPlanner

Type keywords like:

"gift ideas"

"gift ideas for"

"what to give my girlfriend"

"what to give my boyfriend"

"gift for anniversary"

"what to give her"

"what to give him for"

"Christmas gift ideas"

"Best Christmas gifts for her"

Basically, any keyword that hints giving away something.

Enter one or more of the following:

Your product or service

gift ideas for wife

Your landing page

www.example.com/page

Your product category

Enter or select a product category

Targeting [?]

All locations

English

Google

Negative keywords

Date range [?]

Show avg. monthly searches
for: Last 12 months

Customize your search [?]

Keyword filters

Keyword options
Show broadly related ideas
Hide keywords in my account
Hide keywords in my plan

Keywords to include

Get ideas

Your choice of topic is totally up to you.

You can choose to focus on just one demographic, say women. But you can also create a website where's it is like a general gift idea product review site.

Once you hit GET IDEAS.

I want you to sort your competition from LOW TO HIGH

	Ad group ideas	Keyword ideas	

Keyword (by relevance)		Avg. monthly searches ?	Competition ?
valentines for him		3,600	Low
best gifts 2015 for her		260	Low
lesbian gifts		4,400	Low
gift christmas		480	Low
christmas gift guide		2,400	Low
ideas for gift		170	Low
best birthday ideas for wife		70	Low
best christmas present		480	Low
valentines day gifts		14,800	Low
birth gift ideas for wife		10	Low
birthday ideas wife		170	Low
top gifts of 2015		110	Low

These are the keywords that you can target and easily ranked on Google in 1-3 weeks.

Then download these keywords and save it in your desktop.

We will use these later on our content and when we ranked our sites on Google.

2 – Creating a Website

Once you got your keywords, it's time to create a website.

Introducing WordPress…

WHY USE WORDPRESS?

I won't bore you with technical details on why you should use WordPress. The 2 second answer to that is "Google Loves WordPress Sites".
70% of Websites Today That Rank On Google Is WordPress. If that's not enough reason for you to use WordPress then I don't know what to say. ?
Actually I got one more reason. It's super easy to use and build.
 With that being said, let's create your website!

1 - Choose a Domain Name

Go to http://GoDaddy.com and/or http://Internet.bs.
These are the 2 registrar that I used on my 8 previous websites and I haven't experience any problem using them. Feel free to use other domain registrar if you want to.

httpyourbusinessname.com   SEARCH AGAIN

YES! YOUR DOMAIN IS AVAILABLE.
BUY IT BEFORE SOMEONE ELSE DOES.

CONTINUE TO CART

How to choose a proper domain name:
 I would suggest that you use a domain url that is related to your keywords.
Say if your topic is about HOW TO PLAY GUITAR, I would pick something like
Learntoplayguitar.com
Playtheguitar.com
OR
You can also use a brand if you want to.
Just make sure that the brand sounds like it is related to your topic.
Once you've chosen your domain name, click continue to cart and go to checkout to buy it.

2- Website Hosting

You need your own hosting so you'll have full control of your own website. Instead of having a website that looks like www.learnguitar.wordpress.com, you'll have something like this: www.learnguitar.com

In the past, I always recommended HOSTGATOR.com, but I recently got some problem with them and decided to transfer most of my websites to BLUEHOST.COM

If you only have 1 website, I recommend that you start with the cheapest plan which is only $3.95/month.

Got the hosting plan? Great!

3 - CONNECTING NAME SERVERS

Now, we want to connect our GoDaddy account or any domain registrar that we have to our hosting account. We'll do this by connecting "*nameservers*".

Log-in to your GoDaddy account and choose your domain that you've just registered a while ago.

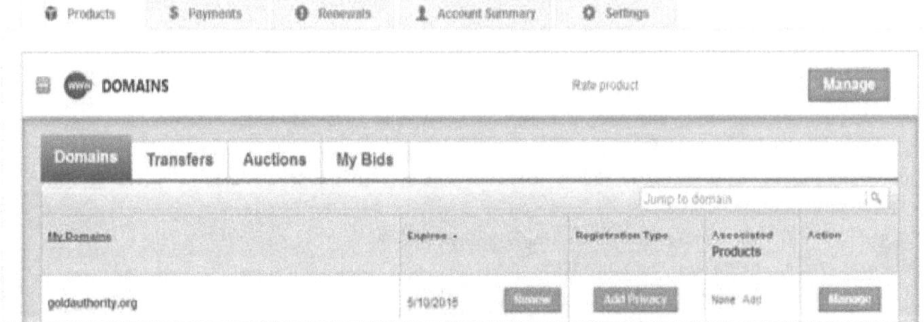

Click Manage. Then Click your website URL.

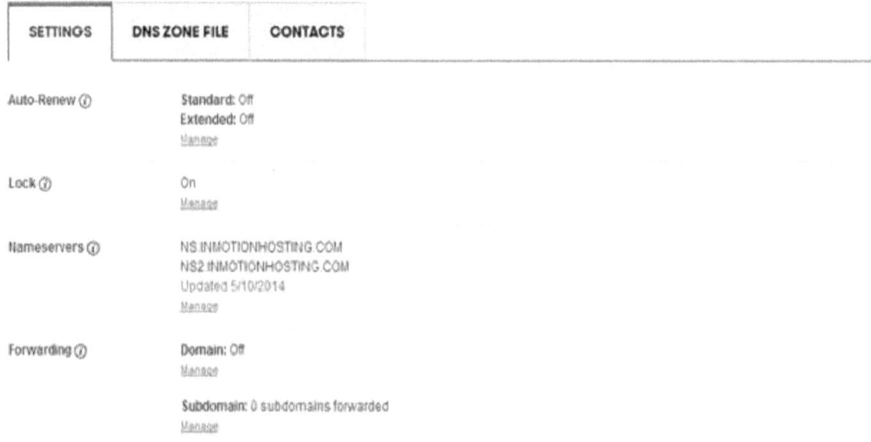

 See the name servers above? Click "Manage" as well.

It will open a small page where you will click "Edit Nameservers"

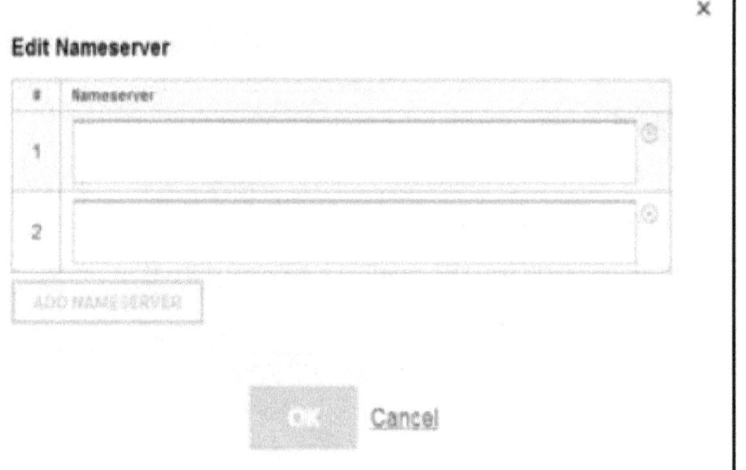

Now, go back to your email address and check for the bluehost cpanel email, you should have received your username and password for this.
Please note that this is different from your BLUEHOST account but sometimes it depends on the hosting company that you use.
If you can't find your cpanel then email your hosting registrar.
Once you log in, you should see your name servers.

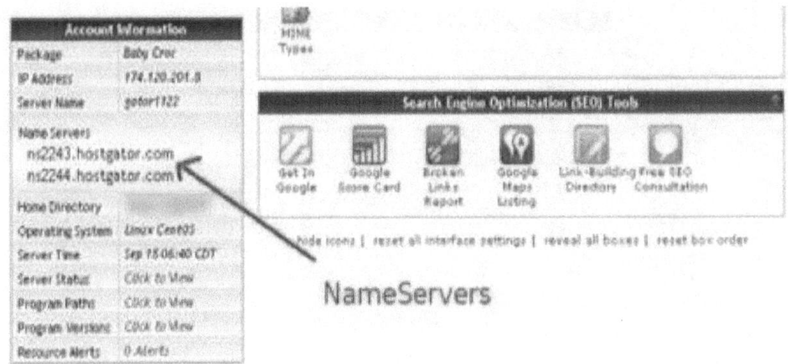

Copy and paste these on the other tab that we just opened a while ago.

Edit Nameserver

#	Nameserver
1	
2	

ADD NAMESERVER

OK   Cancel

Click OK.

Now we are set and we can now install WordPress on our site.

Please take note that sometimes, it may take 24-48 hours for your domain and hosting to connect. But usually, it takes less than 15 minutes.

4 - CPANEL - INSTALL WORDPRESS

Go to your cpanel again and click Fantastico Deluxe or QuickInstall
(Depending on the hosting that you are using, you can also find WORDPRESS directly under SCRIPTS)
Then choose WordPress.
Click Install and Input the necessary details afterwards.
Once you got it installed, go to this link:
http://yoursitename.com/wp-login
Sometimes, it won't load or it will give you an error page.
This simply means your domain and hosting are still "talking" to each other and is still in the process of pagination.
If it gives you the log in page already then go on and log in on your newly installed wordpress site.

5- CHOOSE A THEME
There are tons of FREE wordpress themes to choose from. Depending on the theme of your website, choose something that is related to your topic/blog.
In the **Appearance** tab on the left. Click **Themes.**
Choose the Theme that you want, Click **Add** and Click **Install**

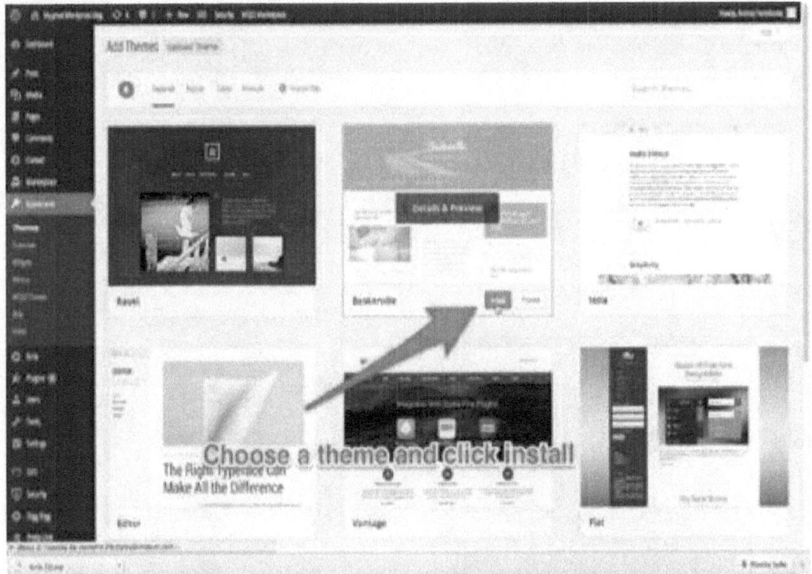
Choose a theme and click Install
The Right Typeface can
Make All the Difference
Baskerville
Editor
Vantage
Flat

PREMIUM WORDPRESS THEME

if you want to install a paid premium theme then this is how you will do it. I recommend using studiopress.com , they have a lot of themes for whatever your site is about (real estate, photography, cake business etc.)

You will receive a zip file from them and you will upload this on your wordpress site.

To do this, hover over APPERANCE and click THEMES.

Then Click Add New

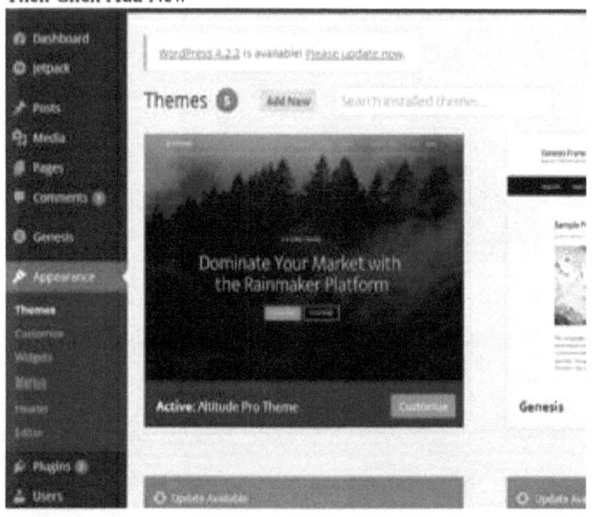

Then click UPLOAD THEME

Choose File and click the file you want to upload.

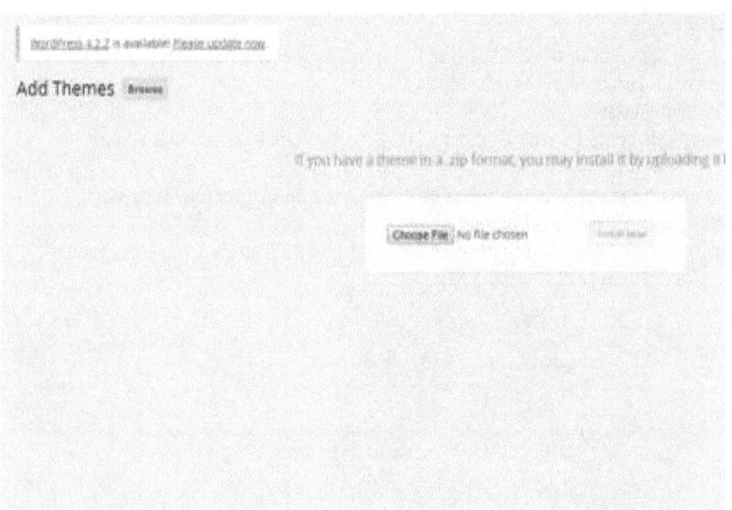

Go back to your themes pages again, see below.
Then Click Activate

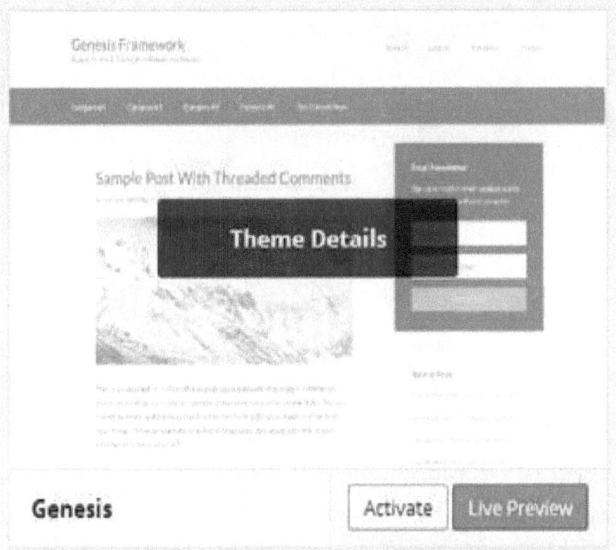

6 - WordPress Set-Up

Now, we will configure your website so GOOGLE will (for that lack of a better word) LIKE IT.
In your WordPress account. Hover in to the left side and
Click on **SETTINGS** then **General.**
Input your website title. This could be your Company Name or the main keyword that you are targeting.
Ex. Let's say that I'm targeting people who are searching for Lasik Surgery in the Philippines. Then I will make my site title "Lasik Surgery Philippines"
For the *Tagline* , I will input and explanation of what the site is about. Then click on save changes below.

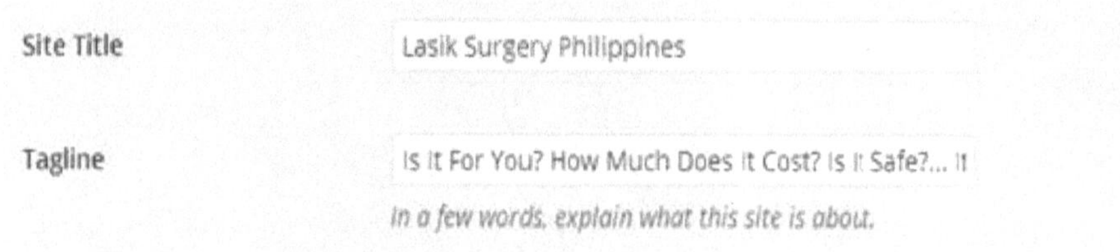

Next, Click on Permalink on the left side of Settings.

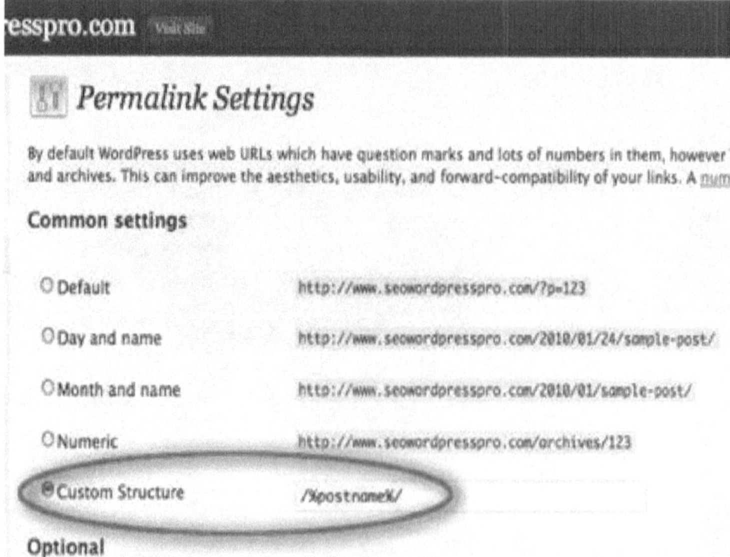

Click "Custom Structure" and type /%postname%/

Or simply click "Post Name" and Save Changes.

Next click the "Pages" tab on the left side of your wordpress admin.

Tick the "sample page" post – select move to trash then APPLY.

7 - Plug-In Set-Up

 Now it's time to install FREE plug-ins that will immensely help us in grabbing google rankings.
Go on the left side of your wordpress admin and click on **PLUGIN.**
Search for these plug ins one by one.

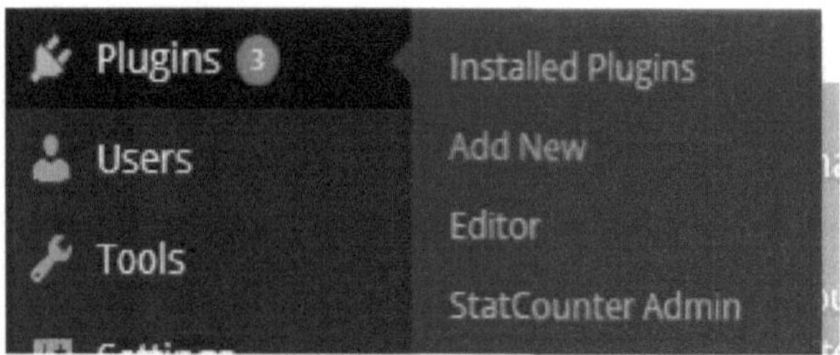

Click ADD NEW and search for these plugins.
1. **Wordpress SEO** – *For OnPage Seo*
2. **W3 Total Cache** – For faster loading websites
3. **Google XML Sitemaps -** *For indexing purposes*
4. **Video XML Sitemap Generator -** *to get easily indexed by Google*
5. **Google Analytics** – Traffic count

Click **INSTALL** and then **ACTIVATE.**

8 – Writing Your First Blog Post

Now that you've got your SEO essentials covered. It's time to put some content on your website. Also, try to embed some youtube videos on your website.

To do this, simply go on your left TAB and click on Post or Pages.

Posts are what normally appear on your homepage and Pages are what appear on different parts of your site.

To create a post, hover over POSTS and click add new.

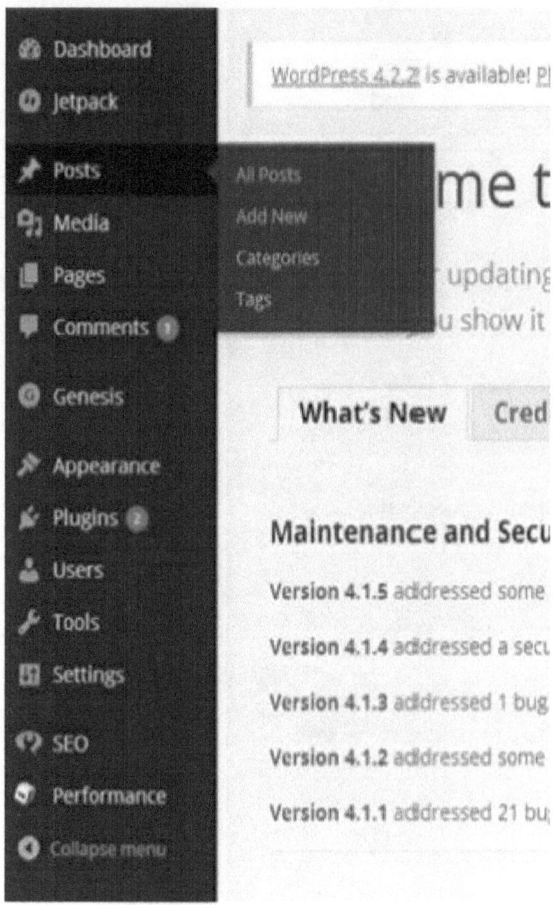

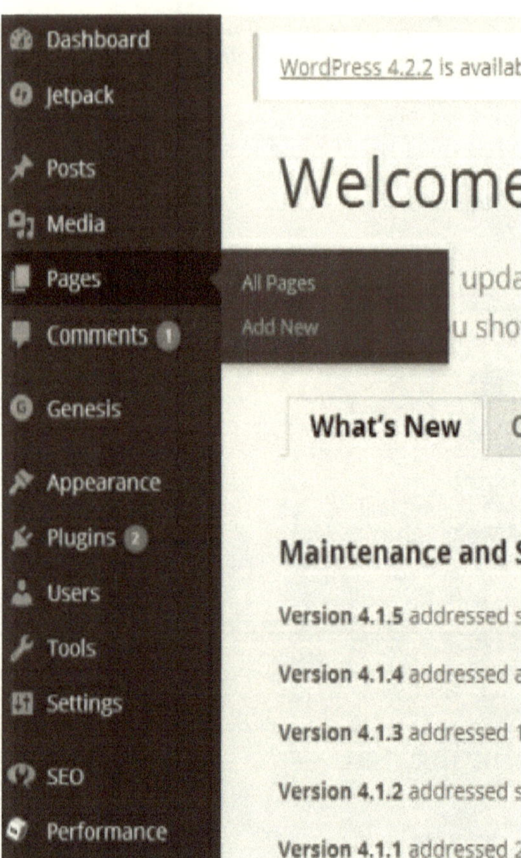

Dashboard
Jetpack
Posts
Media
Pages
Comments
Genesis
Appearance
Plugins
Users
Tools
Settings
SEO
Performance
All Pages
Add New
WordPress 4.2.2 is availab
Welcome
What's New
Maintenance and S
Version 4.1.5 addressed
Version 4.1.4 addressed a
Version 4.1.3 addressed 1
Version 4.1.2 addressed s
Version 4.1.1 addressed 2

To create a new page, hover over PAGES and click add new.

Simply write your content and hit Publish on the right side
Make sure that you have at
least 500 words into it.
Also, try to embed some youtube videos on your website for seo purposes.
You're almost done! To look at your new page or post, once you hit publish, you will see a button on
the upper left that says
"VIEW POST"

HOW TO CREATE AN AWESOME BLOGPOST

Here are some guidelines to follow to make sure that you put some amazing content for your readers.

A- GIVE THEM WHAT THEY WANT

Go to google keywordplanner tool (it's free!) and search for some keywords related to your blog. If
they are searching for guitar lesson for beginners then VOILA!, you now have a topic that they want!

B - SITE SOME PERSONAL EXPERIENCE

People want someone they can related with, not some brass balls guru who knows everything. Yes, you
are the expert but you have to understand that it does not mean that you're untouchable or you never
experienced some failure. Your readers will love you more if they can relate to your stories. Write
about it.

C – NEVER BE AFRAID TO RECOMMEND SOMETHING YOU BELIEVE IN

Most bloggers are afraid because their readers may become upset because they are promoting a product
or a service. If you truly believe that this product can help them achieve their goals and enriched their
lives, then why would you not promote that product? I'm not sure why you want to start a blog but I
would assume that you want to make money and you want to help people at the same time. I say, you
can do both.

Sample post:

To do this, simply go on your left TAB and click on Post or Pages. Posts are what normally appear on your homepage and Pages are what appear on different parts of your site. See image above.

Simply write your content and hit Publish!

Make sure that you have at least 500 words into it.

You're almost done!

But Wait.

BONUS – THE CHECKLIST

Here's a checklist to use so you can make your website and content Google optimized. You don't really need all of them but try to apply as much as possible.

Is your chosen domain short?

Is it memorable?

Is it brandable?

Have you found keywords that are relevant for your business?

Have you chosen a unique main keyword for every page?

Is it purposeful?

Is it long enough to provide users with all the information they're looking for?

Is your main keyword in the main title (H1)?

Have you used your main keyword and variations or synonyms throughout the content?

Have you marked other titles or subtitles with headings?

Have you added your primary keyword into your page URL?

Are you using canonical tags to make sure you don't have any duplicate content?

Does each page on your site include a unique meta title and description?

Do your images have descriptive alt tags and filenames?

Are you linking to your internal pages in an SEO-friendly way?

Have you installed Google Analytics?

Is the website linking to you relevant for your business?

Would you click on that link if it wasn't pointing to your site?

Did you point your social properties (facebook, twitter) to your website?

Did you have at least 500 words on your content?

3 – Write a Product Review

Follow these guidelines when creating your product review.

A.   It should be honest and unbiased

Don't just sell the product for the "sales" sakes.

Give them actual details of what is good about the products and what is bad.

B. Get ideas on Amazon

Go to the product's page itself and read some reviews from actual buyers.

Never write a review without reading at least 3 reviews from the original product page.

You'll know what they like and what they don't like by reading a handful of these reviews first. Also, once you know what they don't like about the product, then you can now think of a good rebuttal and nix their objections.

Read the 5 starts as well as the one star reviews.

Most Helpful Customer Reviews

282 of 294 people found the following review helpful

★★☆☆☆ **Slips when on a wood floor, tore after very first use. Better for general exercise than for yoga.**

By M. Erb #1 HALL OF FAME   TOP 10 REVIEWER   VINE VOICE on July 13, 2014

Length: 1:56 Mins

The Swan Yoga mat comes in 3 colors (red, blue & black.) I received a black yoga mat at no cost for evalutaion. Both my wife and I have been using it for a couple weeks... she does yoga. I use it just as an exercise mat for crunches and general exercise.

This is a fairly thick and squishy mat. It is not at all ideal for Yoga because you don't feel like you are standing firmly. This causes balance issues when doing certain poses, particularly when standing on just one foot. It feels like you're standing on a sponge. I have let several yoga instructors try this mat and they all agree... too soft and squishy and not durable.

Another issue is that the mat slips for my wife when she is doing a pose such as the Downward Dog. You can see in my video how the mat slips and stretches... and it was during that pose on the very first use that the top surface of the mat ripped as well.

I use the mat for crunches and general exercise that doesn't put the kind of stresses on the mat that Yoga poses do. I like the thickness of the mat when doing my crunches as it makes it more comfortable on my lower back and shoulders. Also in side positions where I do leg lifts, the cushiness is nice on the elbows and hip.

I'd say as a Yoga mat this fails. As a general purpose exercise mat, it's pretty good.

6 Comments   Was this review helpful to you?   Yes | No

(pros and cons inside the review below - you can steal the ideas behind this review)

★☆☆☆☆ **Sucked from the start, but I really tried to like it.**
By Ray Smith on May 27, 2015
Color: Dark Green~Green   Verified Purchase

The first thing I noticed when opening my new mat was the smell. The descriptions claims no irritating smell but clearly it stunk. Right now it's sitting out on my front porch to air out while I write my review. Also the product packaging was suspiciously vague and looks very low-quality import style. You know, generic pictures, no company name or information, bad translations that don't really make sense. After recently researching the prevalence of counterfeit products making their way into America from overseas I DO NOT take any claims made by this product page seriously. Who knows exactly what this is made of and why it gives off a strange "plasticky" odor.

I was also suspecting something heavier and denser. When it says lightweight it is not kidding! It's really just a thin piece of textured foam.

So moving past all that I rolled it out to see how it was with slip resistance and whatnot. My first pose was Downward Facing Dog because if there is a pose that will give me trouble with slipping that usually is the culprit. While there was a wee bit of give my hands and feet stayed in place pretty well so I have high hopes that I won't move. If I notice any changes to slip resistance during a sweaty yoga workout I'll update my review.

I was also sad to find a similar mat at Sears for less than $10.

Pros:
- Light to carry
- Doesn't seem to slide
- Appears sturdy

Cons:
- Smells funky
- Suspicious packaging makes me think it came out of a scary Chinese sweatshop
- Isn't really that environmentally friendly (links to research included)
- While researching this brand I found out the Powerextra brand manufactures generic batteries… and then yoga mats. That is just weird to me

Verdict: I'm not going to send it back (yet) but I won't buy another one or suggest it to any of my yoga students. I'm going to continue my search for a sturdy, sticky yoga mat that I fall in love with.

Things I found while researching this mat:
http://ecoyogini.blogspot.com/2011/02/ecoyoga-review-kulae-tpe-ecomat.html
http://www.care2.com/greenliving/tpe-and-sustainable-yoga-mats.html
http://local.sears.com/Shock-Athletic-mm-Reversible-Yoga-Mat-Aqua/p-00615640000P?st=1121&sid=IDx20141117x00001xiplatV

C. Always write the Pros and the Cons

Do not oversell the product. All products has pros and cons, your job is to make the pros weigh higher in their decisions scales.

When you write your cons, make sure that it's not a deal killer. Again, you'll know these things once you start reading actual reviews of the product.

D. Call to Action

Put an affiliate link in the beginning of your review as well at the end.

Also, always hide your affiliate link behind terms like…

'" Click here to visit Amazon's website"

" Click here to see 250 reviews from happy customers"

or add a picture like this:

It should link out to your Amazon affiliate link.

Insert/edit link ✕

Enter the destination URL

URL | http://affiliatelink...

Title |

☐ Open link in a new window/tab

Or link to existing content ▾

Cancel   Add Link

Chapter 7 - Keys to a successful affiliate site

Here are some guidelines to follow for you create a successful affiliate website.

1.Compelling and Relevant Content

At the moment that they land in your website, you should make them feel that your website got what they need.

If you just outsourced your content, make sure that he/she doesn't mention any current events that may be outdated by the time they see that content.

2. SEO Tags

These are the h1, h2 tags in your content.

So if a certain page is about " LXM guitar reviews", then put

<h1> Best Guitar Reviews</h1> on the title.

This lets Google know that your website or that content is specifically about LXM Guitar reviews… get what I mean? Awesome.

An h2 tag indicates that a certain term is also related to your topic.

<h2> LXM Guitar Reviews </h2>

Use h1 and h2 only once per post/page.

Don't use the same h2 tags repeatedly even in different pages.

3. Outbound Links

Outbound links are basically website that you refer to in your content.

Let's say you are talking about "guitar reviews" , you'll then link out to

guitarcenter.com (which is an atuhority when it comes to guitars) ex.   I was at <u>guitar center</u> a month ago when I saw this tiny guitar.

4. Unbiased , Honest Reviews

On chapter 7, I taught you how to create a compelling review.

Make sure that you follow the steps and guidelines that I showed you in that chapter.

Just make sure that your reviews are unbiased and honest.

Also, never ever promote a product that just scammed people, no matter how big the pay is.

4 – Ranking in Google

If you did the keyword research method that I taught you, then you won't have any problems ranking your website on Google's page 1.

First of all, ranking on page 1 of Google takes a little bit of time these days. It may take a new site 30-60 days to get on Page 1. But if you have chosen an uncompetitive niche, then you can rank in less than 30 days.

Method #1 - Fiverr

You can find someone on Fiverr to send backlinks to your website.

You'll simply give the keywords that you want to rank for and the url of your affiliate site.

They'll do everything else for you.

And you're done for this chapter… now, let's do some youtube magic which is basically the same process but just a bit different .. just a bit.

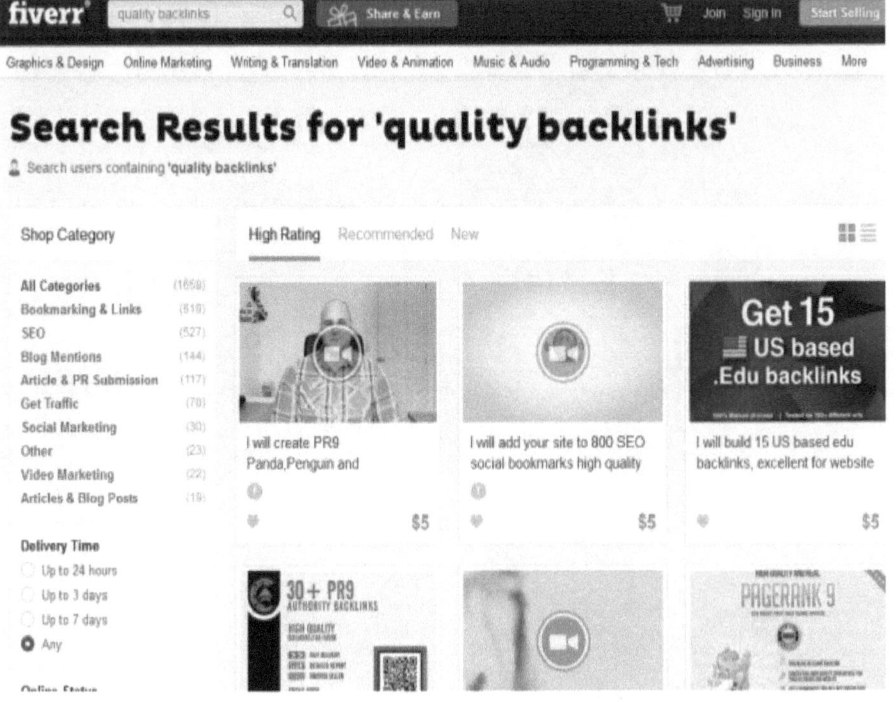

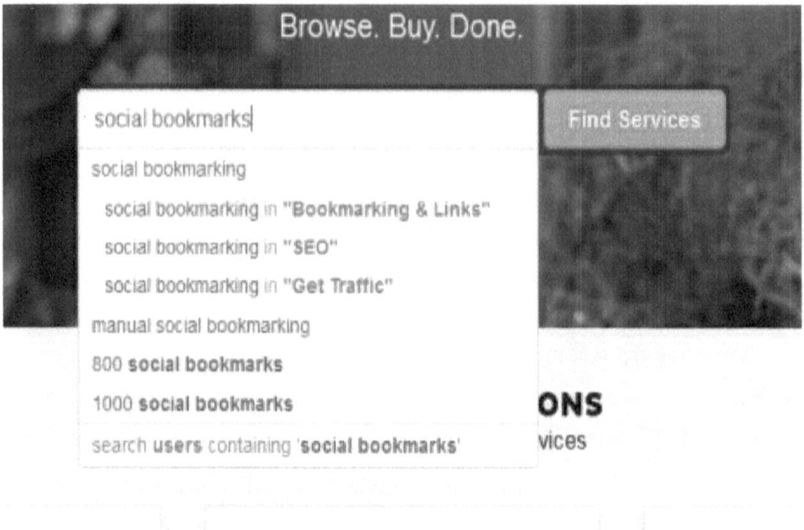

Browse. Buy. Done.
social bookmarks
Find Services
social bookmarking
social bookmarking in "Bookmarking & Links"
social bookmarking in "SEO"
social bookmarking in "Get Traffic"
manual social bookmarking
800 social bookmarks
1000 social bookmarks
search users containing 'social bookmarks'
ONS
vices

Method # 2 - Youtube Videos

This is the easiest way of getting visitors to your website. Videos are 10X easier to rank on Google compared to websites.

Follow this simple process to rank your youtube video on Google.

Step 1 - Create a video review of the product you want to promote.

You may need to buy the product yourself or do a powerpoint presentation where you record your screen.

Step 2 - Upload on youtube

Follow this guidelines when uploading your youtube video.

A. Title

Your title should have the exact keyword phrase you are targeting.

B. Short and Sweet

If you can make your video length, 5 minutes or less the better. No one really watches long videos on youtube except if it is a documentary or if it is about something they are really interested in.

C. File name

Make sure that you file name has your main keyword in it.

Ex. Bestfibersupplement.mov

The Google algorithm loves it when a file name is related to your video content because it let Google know that the video is about that topic.

It's like you're saying

"Hey Mr. G!, my video is about fiber supplements!"

And then Mr. G answers back – "Thanks men, I will reward you for that – I will give you higher google rankings!"

OK, this is getting weird but I know that you get the point.

D. Title Stacking

Putting your keyword twice in the title will help your google rankings.

Make sure though that your title makes sense and you're not just spamming the crap out of youtube.

Ex.

Fiber Supplements Review – The Best Fiber Supplements of 2015

It repeats your keyword fiber supplements but with variation, by adding "Review" and "The best" + "2015".

E. Your channel name

Your channel name should be related to your keyword as much as possible.

Ex. Main keyword is "fiber supplement reviews"

Your channel name could be –

SupplementsReviewChannel

TheSupplementReviewer

Fibersupplementsreview

Just pick something that has some of your keywords in it.

F. Tag Ripping

Find the most competitive and related videos to yours and copy their tags.

For instance, say your keyword term is "fiber supplement reviews." Go and search the term in YouTube and see which videos come up. Then copy all the tags from the top 3 videos.

These people just did all the hard work for you! You just copy and paste all of their tags plus you never really have to do any grunt work.

G. Description

One of the most important parts of your video is your description. It has three purposes.

First, it let the viewers know what it is they are watching.

Second, you can use it to link out to your website or to any website where you want your viewers to go

Third, it helps Google in determining what the content is about. It also helps in rankings since it is part of Youtube-Google algorithm.

You must put http:// on your url to make it clickable.

Today, I recommend that you put a 250 words description on your video. Tell them what they can expect in the video and put your website link on it.

Step 3 - Fiverr

SInce youtube is a bit different than Google, we can just hire someone on Fiverr to send links to our youtube video to get it ranked on Google.

Send backlinks to your video

The old way is to directly send tons of spammy links to your video. This still works sometimes but Youtube is now catching up.

To counter this, we just need to send the links to a url shortener instead of sending it directly to our youtube page.

I just use https://bitly.com and put my videolink, it'll generate a new url.

You can send your backlinks in this new url.

If you want, you can tell your outsourcer to send half the backlinks on your bitly url and half on your original video url.

On fiverr, search for backlinks and find someone who can send social bookmarks or any social links to your url.

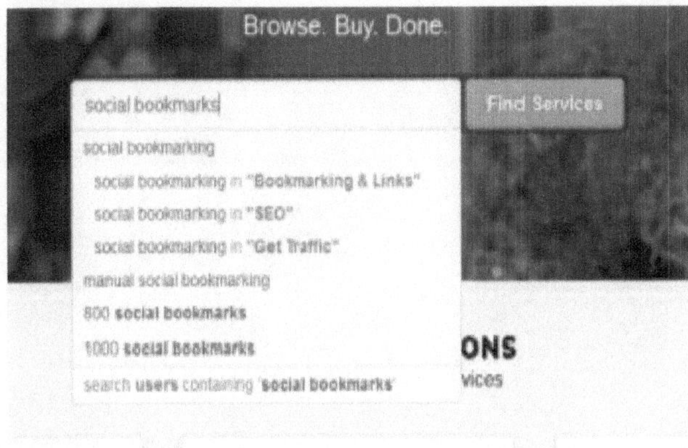

You'll see your video ranked on first page in 3-4 weeks.

Conclusion

Good job!

You finished the book and you're on your way to making some awesome part-time income that could also be passive income once you got your whole process figured out.

The next step is scaling it and hiring other people to do the keyword research, website creation and all the other parts for you.

But let's not get ahead of ourselves.

For now, try to create your own website and learn to write reviews and rank them on Google.Good luck brother! (or sister :p),

AFFILIATE QUICK BUCK

The Fastest Way To Make Huge Affiliate Commission Online

Jonathan Parker & Andre Bennet

THE BIG PROMISE:

I WILL SHOW YOU THE FASTEST WAY TO EARN AFFILIATE COMMISSIONS ONLINE

Table of Contents

Introduction

Let's get straight to the point. You downloaded this book you want a simple and fast way to make money online.

The system that you'll learn is all about using a system called LAUNCH JACKING. It basically means promoting product launches ..more specifically INFORMATION PRODUCTS or COURSES.

Promoting these kind of offers will make us money faster because product launches already have abig demand. Your job is to make sure that you are in front of that demand when the launch happens.

I will teach you everything you need to know to have a successful LJ campaign.

Just follow my step by step website creation instructions and make sure that you choose the right product launch.

I won't try to bullshit you just to make this book longer, so let's get started already.

Step To Making Money

Here's the whole system in a nutshell.

1 – Find A Profitable Product Launch

The first step is to find a product that we want to promote. It's important to choose a product launch with reputable product creators. We don't just promote a product just because it has a high commission. Remember, if you promote a crap product, your customers will shit it back to you.

2- Create Your Website

This part is a bit techie, but I found a simple way to teach you how to create a website. We''ll just gonna use Wordpress.

3 – Write An Amazing Product Review

Once they landed on your website, your content must immediately pre-sell your customers to your product;that's why you need to write a compelling review.

4 – Give Amazing Bonuses

One of the most important aspect of a successful product launch is the bonus giveaway. Give the right type of bonus can easily double or triple your income.

5 – Rank Your Website on the 1st page of Google

Everything is set. One last step is to rank your website on Google's 1st page. Also, we have to choose the keywords that we want to rank for.

The next step is to rinse and repeat the process to make more money.

Chapter 1 - Product Launches

So where do we find those profitable products? Well, here are my most favorite sources of product launches. Some items will be crap so we have to make sure that we chose a reputable product creator. After I gave you the product launch sources, I'll teach you my guidelines on choosing a product to promote.

Product Niches:

There's a lot of niches out there, but my favorite niches to promote a product with are:

Weight Loss

Muscle Gain

Relationship & Dating Advice

General Internet Marketing

Real Estate

Stock Market

Forex

Product Sources:

1 - CLICKBANK

The normal way to find product is through the CB market place. That's awesome and you should do that. **The first thing that I suggest you do is to sign up as an affiliate to MOST if not all the product with at least a gravity of 50.** If you are in their mailing list, you'll be one of the few people to know if there will be a new product that they will launch. You don't have to promote their current product. Also, don't be obsessed about it asking when is the next product launch. Just sign up as their affiliate and move on for now. When they have a new product, they will surely email their affiliate about it. The great thing about this method is that most of the product creators are always launching or relaunching new products every now and then. These guys are internet marketers, not just product creators.

http://www.clickbank.com/index.html

Search for a niche, ex. Weight loss, then arrange it by gravity. The higher the gravity, means the more people making money in it.

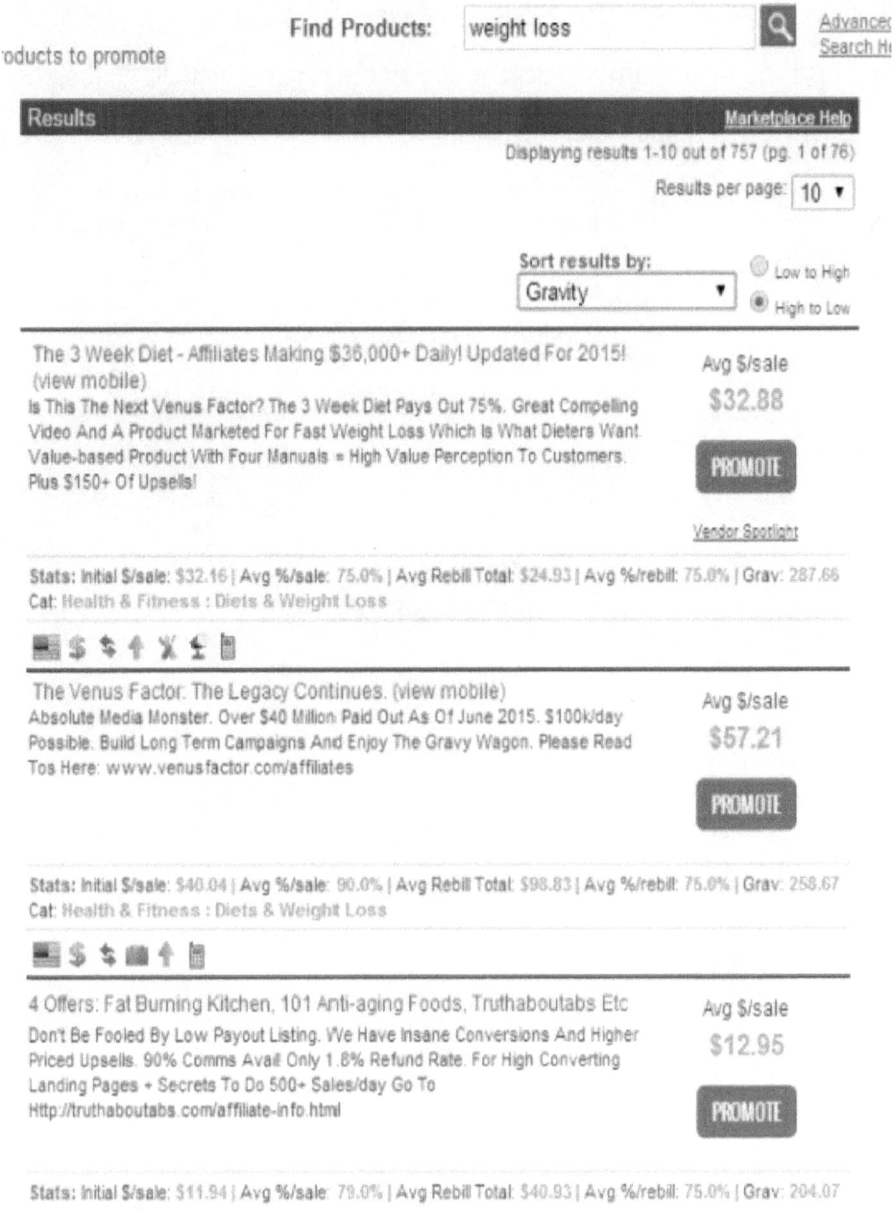

Find Products: weight loss   Advanced
Search H

Results   Marketplace Help

Displaying results 1-10 out of 757 (pg. 1 of 76)

Results per page: 10 ▼

Sort results by:
Gravity ▼   ○ Low to High
                   ● High to Low

The 3 Week Diet - Affiliates Making $36,000+ Daily! Updated For 2015! (view mobile)
Is This The Next Venus Factor? The 3 Week Diet Pays Out 75%. Great Compelling Video And A Product Marketed For Fast Weight Loss Which Is What Dieters Want. Value-based Product With Four Manuals = High Value Perception To Customers. Plus $150+ Of Upsells!

Avg $/sale
$32.88

PROMOTE

Vendor Spotlight

Stats: Initial $/sale: $32.16 | Avg %/sale: 75.0% | Avg Rebill Total: $24.93 | Avg %/rebill: 75.0% | Grav: 287.66
Cat: Health & Fitness : Diets & Weight Loss

The Venus Factor: The Legacy Continues. (view mobile)
Absolute Media Monster. Over $40 Million Paid Out As Of June 2015. $100k/day Possible. Build Long Term Campaigns And Enjoy The Gravy Wagon. Please Read Tos Here: www.venusfactor.com/affiliates

Avg $/sale
$57.21

PROMOTE

Stats: Initial $/sale: $40.04 | Avg %/sale: 90.0% | Avg Rebill Total: $98.83 | Avg %/rebill: 75.0% | Grav: 258.67
Cat: Health & Fitness : Diets & Weight Loss

---

4 Offers: Fat Burning Kitchen, 101 Anti-aging Foods, Truthaboutabs Etc
Don't Be Fooled By Low Payout Listing. We Have Insane Conversions And Higher Priced Upsells. 90% Comms Avail Only 1.8% Refund Rate. For High Converting Landing Pages + Secrets To Do 500+ Sales/day Go To Http://truthaboutabs.com/affiliate-info.html

Avg $/sale
$12.95

PROMOTE

Stats: Initial $/sale: $11.94 | Avg %/sale: 79.0% | Avg Rebill Total: $40.93 | Avg %/rebill: 75.0% | Grav: 204.07

Open a website.

http://www.3weekdiet.com/?hop=0

Look at the bottom and click the text that says AFFILIATES.

It'll take you to their affiliate page where you can sign up in their mailing list.

http://www.3weekdiet.com/affiliates.html

Get started today by creating your referral link below. You can then use some of the tools we have provided (banners, articles, emails) to help promote The 3 Week Diet. Let us know if you need anything at anytime. We are happy to help you.

Then repeat the process to other websites and niches.

2 – JVNOTIFYPRO

Most if not all the product here are about making money online – or mostly about internet marketing.

Go sign up for a free account here:
http://v3.jvnotifypro.com/account/
What I like about JVNotifyPro is that they never seem to run out of product launches. Which is good and bad. Good, because we never have to worry about running out of products to promote. Bad because the market may get tired of the product launches. But you don't have to worry, as long as you are choosing the right product launches.

3 - MUNCHEYE

http://muncheye.com/

There is a shit ton of product to promote here. But it still a good resource for getting news about the largest product launches in the marketing scene.

4 – NETWORK YOUR ASS OFF

I know that you are suppose to be an internet marketer, living the dream, working at the beach, never seeing a lot of people. But right now, especially if you're just starting out, throw that bullshit away. If you want to get the BEST, and I mean, the very best product creators online, then you have to come to them. It would also be really nice if you personally know the product creator, because you'll know that he won't provide crap to your potential buyers. I've said this before and I'll say it again. Promote crap...and they will shit it back to you.

There are a lot of internet marketing events out there. You don't have to spend $10,000 for a 3 day seminar. There are $1,000 3 day seminars out there which are really good. Their content is probably... ok, but what you're really after for these events are the contacts. Go network your ass off, don't be the shy guy. You need to learn how to talk to people, introduce yourself and tell them what you do. You'll be shocked at how many people will be willing to give you a head up about their coming launches. You'll also get to meet product creators from various niches like dog training, dating, self defense, singing etc. So you don't have to focus with just the internet marketing niche, which is pretty crowded anyway.

5 – The non obvious obvious way

Another super easy way to find product launches is to Google it. I know, seems obvious, but a lot of people don't do it!

Just choose a niche and then type product launch.

Ex.

Forex product launches

Real estate investing course product launch

Then just dig dip. Eventually, you'll find a good product launch.

6 - WARRIOR FORUM

There's a lot of know it all people inside this forum. Be careful when choosing to participate in a thread. Just be friendly and provide helpful content to your co-warriors. Although a lot of trolls are lurking the forum, you can still meet a lot of good and honest people here.
Here are some of my guidelines when choosing a launch to promote:

These are just, well, guidelines. You don't have to follow each and every one of them. But these could give you a pretty good idea of what kind of launches to promote and what not.

1 – He must be a really cool dude. Seriously, if I seem him yapping on facebook about refunds. I'll double think about promoting him. Refunds are part of the business anyway.

2 – For beginners, At least a commission of $30 per sale. If it's a recurring product, I won't mind making $10 per sale, as long as I'm making another $10 per month...till eternity..or till he unsubscribe.

3 – For advance marketers, commission should $100 bucks per sale.

4 – There should be upsells (but not too much – 2 is fine). Two week ago, I saw a guy that has something like 20 upsells, Seriously, I'm not kidding. What a prick.

5 – There should be a very good sales video or sales letter.

6 – It should not be his first product launch.

7 – The product should genuinely help people.

8 – The launch shouldn't be in at least the next 4 weeks you you'll still have time to rank your website, create content and all that stuff.
Chapter 2 - Your Website

For you to sell those products, you will need to create a website. Fortunately, it's super easy!

1 - Choose a Domain Name

Go to http://GoDaddy.com and/or http://Internet.bs.
These are the 2 registrar that I used on my 8 previous websites and I haven't experience any problem using them. Feel free to use other domain registrar if you want to.

How to choose a proper domain name:

 I would suggest that you use a domain url that is related to your keywords.
Say if your product is called YOUTUBE FAST CASH, I would pick something like
youtubefastcashreview.com
youtubefastcashscam.com

2- Website Hosting

You need your own hosting so you'll have full control of your own website. Instead of having a website that looks like www.learnguitar.wordpress.com, you'll have something like this:

www.learnguitar.com

In the past, I always recommended HOSTGATOR.com, but I recently got some problem with them and decided to transfer most of my websites to BLUEHOST.COM

If you only have 1 website, I recommend that you start with the cheapest plan which is only $3.95/month.

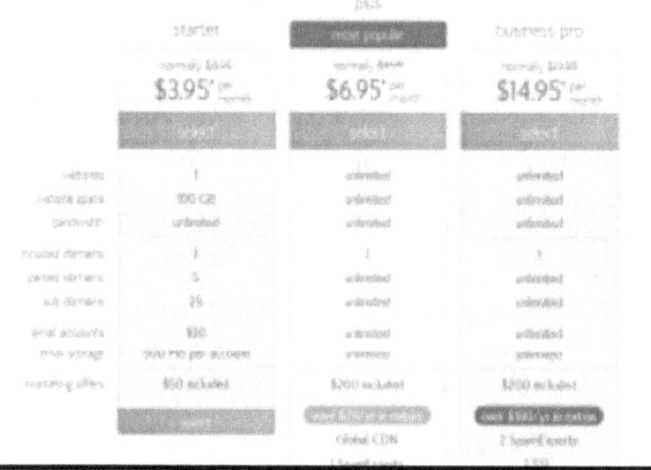

Got the hosting plan? Great!

3 - CONNECTING NAME SERVERS

Now, we want to connect our GoDaddy account or any domain registrar that we have to our hosting account. We'll do this by connecting *"nameservers"*.

Log-in to your GoDaddy account and choose your domain that you've just registered a while ago.

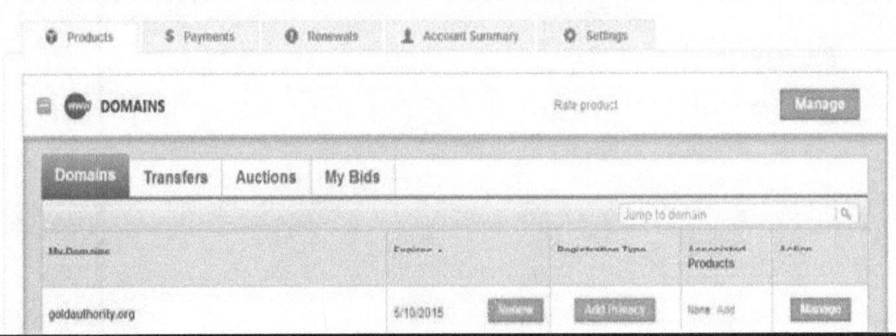

Click Manage. Then Click your website URL.

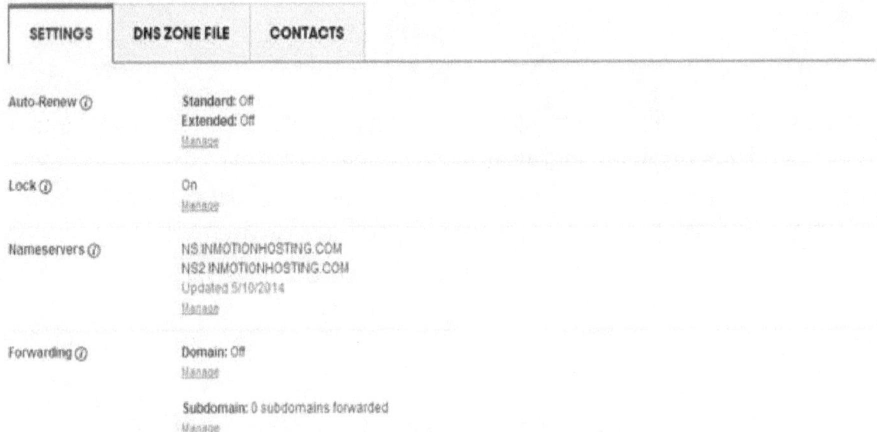

 See the name servers above? Click "Manage" as well.

It will open a small page where you will click "Edit Nameservers"

Edit Nameserver

Now, go back to your email address and check for the bluehost cpanel email, you should have received your username and password for this.
Please note that this is different from your BLUEHOST account but sometimes it depends on the hosting company that you use.
If you can't find your cpanel then email your hosting registrar.
Once you log in, you should see your name servers.

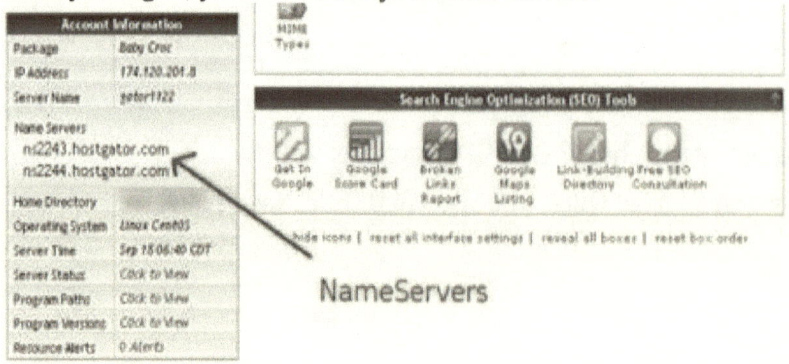

Copy and paste these on the other tab that we just opened a while ago.

Click OK.

Now we are set and we can now install WordPress on our site.

Please take note that sometimes, it may take 24-48 hours for your domain and hosting to connect. But usually, it takes less than 15 minutes.

4 - CPANEL - INSTALL WORDPRESS

Go to your cpanel again and click Fantastico Deluxe or QuickInstall

(Depending on the hosting that you are using, you can also find WORDPRESS directly under SCRIPTS)

Then choose WordPress.

Click Install and Input the necessary details afterwards.

Once you got it installed, go to this link:
http://yoursitename.com/wp-login
Sometimes, it won't load or it will give you an error page.
This simply means your domain and hosting are still "talking" to each other and is still in the process of pagination.
If it gives you the log in page already then go on and log in on your newly installed wordpress site.

5- CHOOSE A THEME

There are tons of FREE wordpress themes to choose from. Depending on the theme of your website, choose something that is related to your topic/blog.
In the **Appearance** tab on the left. Click **Themes.**
Choose the Theme that you want, Click **Add** and Click **Install**

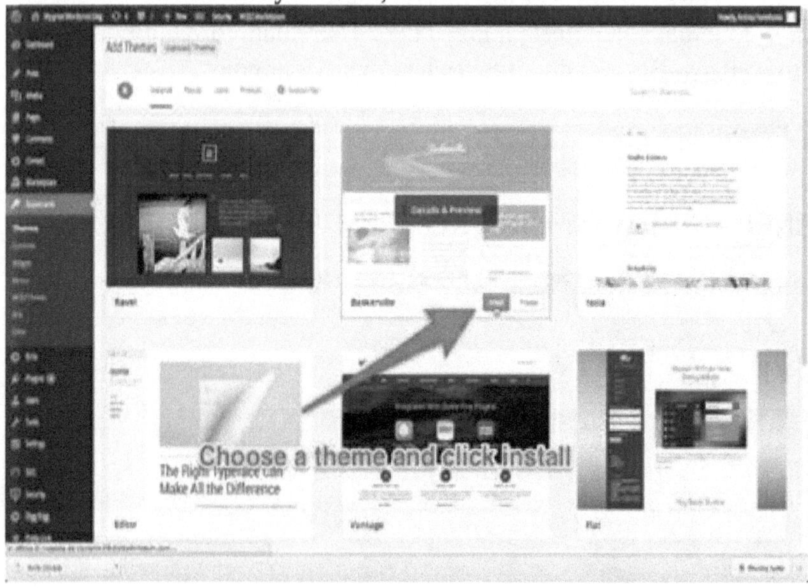

PREMIUM WORDPRESS THEME

if you want to install a paid premium theme then this is how you will do it. I recommend using studiopress.com , they have a lot of themes for whatever your site is about (real estate, photography, cake business etc.)

You will receive a zip file from them and you will upload this on your wordpress site.

To do this, hover over APPERANCE and click THEMES.

Then Click Add New

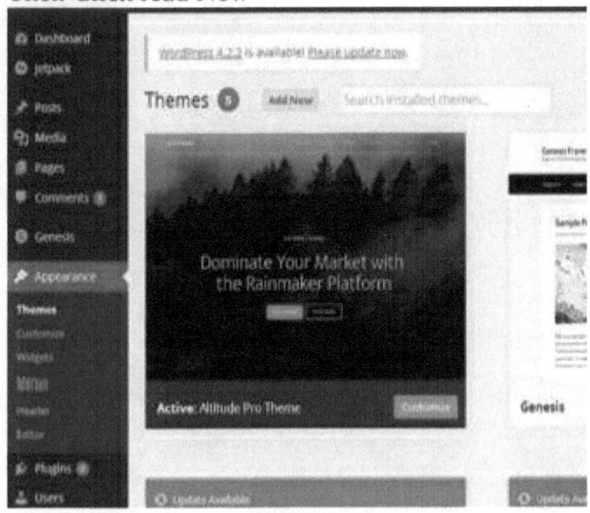

Then click UPLOAD THEME

Choose File and click the file you want to upload.

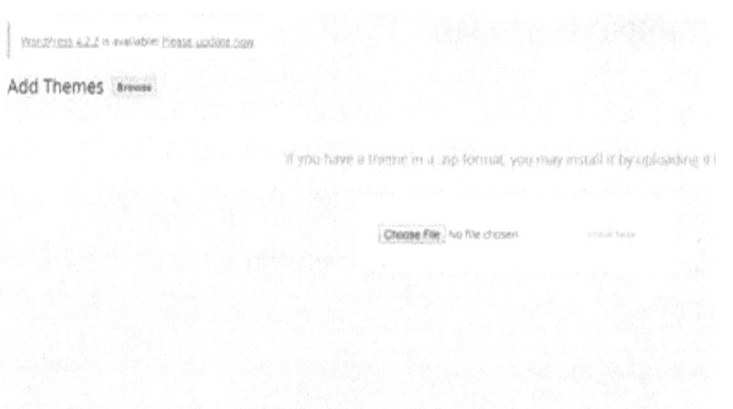

Go back to your themes pages again, see below.
Then Click Activate

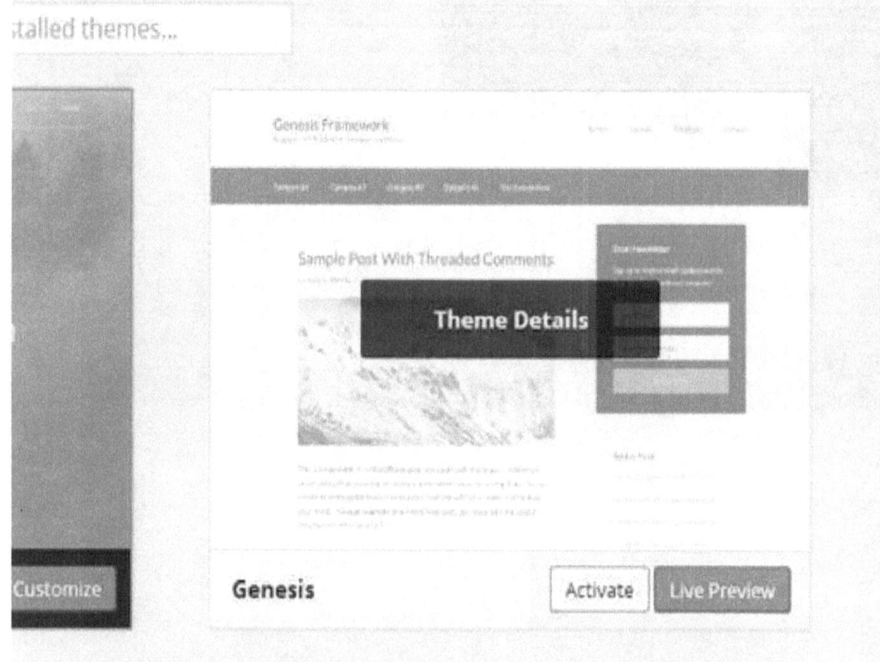

6 - WordPress Set-Up

Now, we will configure your website so GOOGLE will (for that lack of a better word) LIKE IT.

In your WordPress account. Hover in to the left side and

Click on **SETTINGS** then **General.**

Input your website title. This could be your Company Name or the main keyword that you are targeting.

Ex. Let's say that I'm targeting people who are searching for Lasik Surgery in the Philippines. Then I will make my site title "Lasik Surgery Philippines"

For the *Tagline* , I will input and explanation of what the site is about. Then click on save changes below.

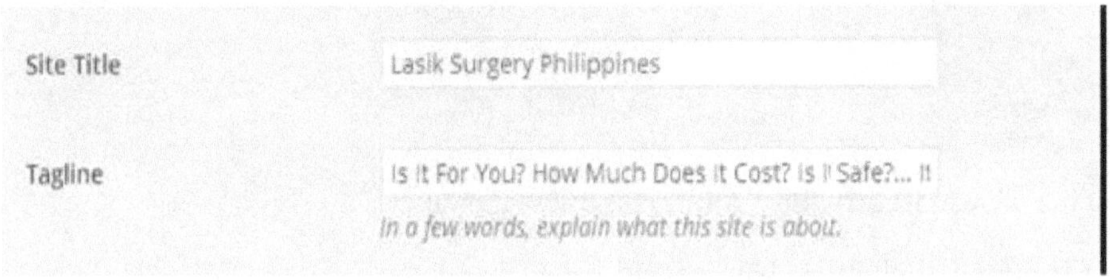

Site Title	Lasik Surgery Philippines
Tagline	Is It For You? How Much Does It Cost? Is It Safe?... It
	In a few words, explain what this site is about.

Next, Click on Permalink on the left side of Settings.

Permalink Settings

By default WordPress uses web URLs which have question marks and lots of numbers in them, however and archives. This can improve the aesthetics, usability, and forward-compatibility of your links. A num

Common settings

Optional

Click "Custom Structure" and type /%postname%/

Or simply click "Post Name" and Save Changes.

Next click the "Pages" tab on the left side of your wordpress admin. Tick the "sample page" post – select move to trash then APPLY.

7 - Plug-In Set-Up

Now it's time to install FREE plug-ins that will immensely help us in grabbing google rankings.

Go on the left side of your wordpress admin and click on **PLUGIN.**

Search for these plug ins one by one.

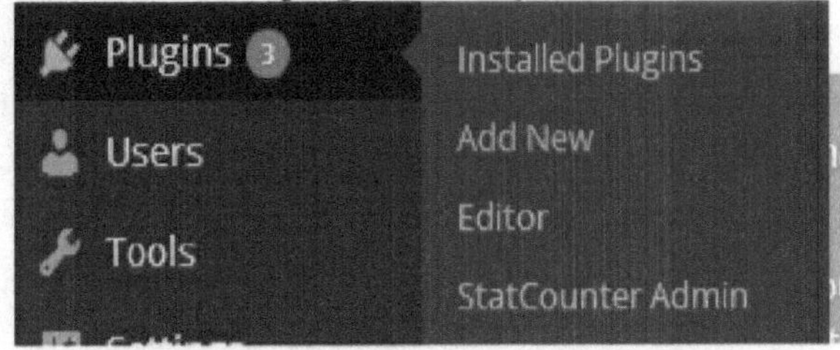

Click ADD NEW and search for these plugins.

1. **Wordpress SEO** – *For OnPage Seo*
2. **W3 Total Cache** – For faster loading websites
3. **Google XML Sitemaps** - *For indexing purposes*
4. **Video XML Sitemap Generator** - *to get easily indexed by Google*
5. **Google Analytics** – Traffic count

Click **INSTALL** and then **ACTIVATE.**

Chapter 3 – Product Reviews That Sell

I have no specific formula or method to give you for writing your reviews. What I have are must include, must follow guidelines whenever you are writing one.

When you are writing your review, try to avoid getting over hyped or being too good to be true. Just be honest in your review, if there's one thing that you don't like about the product, then tell it. Unless it seems like a deal killer, then that's when you should think twice about putting it in your review. But again, be honest, trust me – your customers will appreciate you more if you are honest with your reviews. You do them right, they give the favor back to you.

The Guidelines:

1 - If you can review the product module by module, do it.

2 - Always write the pros and the cons. Tell them what you like and what you don't.

3 – Give a brief overview of the product creator

4 - Always provide an exclusive bonus

5 – You can create a new page just for your bonuses if the review is too long

6 – Always ask for an action. A call to action should always be at least in the beginning or middle and end of your review.

7 – Put a P.S. – where you will give another call to action. Always give them a reason to click the link.

8 – Make your product review clean looking. Which means put it on a 1 page plain looking website. There's no need for massive web design. A simple 1 page review would be enough.

9 – If you could do a video review (where your just reading or reinstating your written review) do it.

10 – If you have a log in access. You could also show a tour of the members area and show them what they will get if they join.

11- Mention an announcement or a special bonus for the first 5-10 people who will buy from your link. It give them a reason to act quickly and buy the product before any one else gets your special bonus.

Here's an example website where you could model your review:

http://www.viperchill.com/source-phoenix-review/ - click the link to checkout the full review.

Last Updated: Thursday 30th October 2014

If you've been involved in the internet marketing world for more than a few months then undoubtedly you'll be receiving emails and seeing Facebook updates about the soon to launch **Source Phoenix** from Alex Becker of Source Wave fame.

One of the cool things about any product launch in the marketing and SEO world is that the author puts a *lot* of effort into the "pre-launch". They want to show you how smart and knowledgeable they are on a topic before they sell you something.

So for the next week Alex is going to be sharing really informative videos on the topic of SEO. If you want to skip this review and go check them out, you can do so here.

So who's behind Source Pheonix?

Chapter 4 - Bonuses

Your bonuses can make or break your attempt to make money on these launches. Depending on the commission of the product that you are promoting, you may want to consider giving away these bonuses. Why these products? Because consumers like it. Don't argue, they just do. Also, I will assume that you are no big name guru who has lots of products available to be given as bonuses. So, we can't compete with them in that category, but we can provide something they already want.

1 – Ipad/Ipad Mini

2 – Anything New From Apple

3- Kindle Reader

4 - Amazon Echo

5 – Best Seller Books with FREE SHIPPING

6 – 1 hour - 1 on1 consultation

Even if you are just a beginner, you'll probably know some things that you can share to your customers. Give them an hour of your time to help them with whatever their problem is.

7 – Backlinks Package

You can hire someone on Fiverr for $10 to provide this package for you. You don't have to tell them that you'll be the one doing it, I doubt that they'll ask about it anyway.

Chapter 5 - Search Engine Optimization

Before you rank your website, you have to know what keywords to rank for first.These should be the keywords that customers are typing to search for the product.

Simply follow these formulas when choosing your keywords.

Product name + reviews

Product name + review

Product name + bonus

Product name + scam

Product creator's name + product name

Product creator's name + product name review

Product creator's name + scam

 So if your chosen product name is

" YOUTUBE FAST CASH BY ERNIE JAMES", your keywords would be…

YOUTUBE FAST CASH review

YOUTUBE FAST CASH reviews

Youtube Fast Cash scam?

Youtube Fast Cash ERNIE JAMES

ERNIE JAMES

ERNIE JAMES Youtube Fast Cash

Youtube Fast Cash Bonus

Ranking Your Website:
There are 3 ways that I used to ranked my product launch sites.

1- FIVERR

If it's a big launch, I will spend a minimum of $100 on backlinks from Fiverr.
Also I will mix it with the second method.
To find backlinks on Fiverr by searching for:
Backlinks
Social backlinks
PBN backlinks
Social bookmarking
Article blast
IFTT links
I will usually chose sellers with 4 or 5 stars.
That's all to it really, you just give him your website url and the keywords
you want to rank for.

2- YOUTUBE VIDEOS
I will also create a youtube video about:
- A video reviewing the product
- A video reviewing the pre-launch content
- A video reviewing the product and giving away the bonuses

This will give you more eyeballs in your offer. Just make sure that you put
your website url below the videos.
Also, this will be helpful SEO wise, youtube is a trusted partner of Google
(Google owns it), and it'll give you a ranking boost.

3 – FIX YOUR ON PAGE SEO
It's not all about the backlinks. Your on page seo will have a HUGE impact
on your sites 1st page ranking or demise.
I got this from chapter 6 of my new book **ON PAGE SEO that doesn't
suck**. The examples are about texas bbq and guitar lessons but you can still
apply it to your product launch websites.
URL/Title Relationship

Consider this lesson as one of the most important part of ON PAGE SEO. This alone could help you rank your website...but it could also ruin your chances if you do it wrong.

Alright. Let's say you are targeting the keyword ONLINE GUITAR LESSONS FOR BEGINNERS.

Then you created a page about it with the same title.
If your website url is a brand name, then it is ok if the extension words are also brandname.com/**ONLINEGUITARLESSONSFORBEGINNERS.**

However, if your website url is already like something close to these (url that already has the keywords in it)…

www.guitarlessons.com
www.onlineguitar.com
www.onlineguitarlessonsforbeginners.com

I suggest that you don't put
ONLINEGUITARLESSONSFORBEGINNERS as your url extension. A website like this,
www.onlineguitarlessonsforbeginners.com/**ONLINEGUITARLESSONSEO**
, will be subject for over optimization. I can almost guarantee you that your website will get penalized.

Another example,...cause you know. I love you. Ok, sorry - I think I've been writing for like 4 hours straight.

Anyway, another example would be this one.

If you have a website about texasbbq and your url is Tomassauce.com

You can use the TITLE (TEXAS BBQ) and the URL (Tomassauce.com/texasbbq) at the same time.

However, if your url is already TEXASBBQ.COM and your targeting
TEXAS BBQ in Google. You should not use the url
TEXASBBQ.com/texasbbq.

I suggest that you add LSI keywords in your url if you already have an exact
match domain.

So instead of having **texasbbq.com/texasbbq** , use something like

TexasBBQ.com/TXBarbeque

By doing this, You are still getting RELEVANCE power and you can still
use your keyword (TEXASBBQ) as your title.

WAYS TO GET BACKLINKS TO YOUR WEBSITE
RELEVANT BLOGS
The key here is relevant. We want a link that is related to out topic. Go to
Google and search for…
KEYWORDS "powered by wordpress" "leave a comment"
The keywords is your market.
If your market is weight loss, then you should search for something like this.
FAT LOSS "powered by wordpress" "leave a comment"

Try to find high pr wordpress blog where you can comment in.

LEAVE A REPLY

Name (required)

Fatlossforguys

Mail (will not be published) (required)

fatlossforguys@gmail.com

Website

http://yourwebsite.com

Message

Hey there awesome site

Some site allows you to post via facebook too.
You can simply link to your website and that counts as a backlink already.

http://mywebsite.com sample

Also post on Facebook   Post

I recommend that you comment on pr1 sites and above.

INFO GRAPHICS

One of the best ways to spread your content (with a link back to your site) is

to
create a info graphic from piktopchart.com.

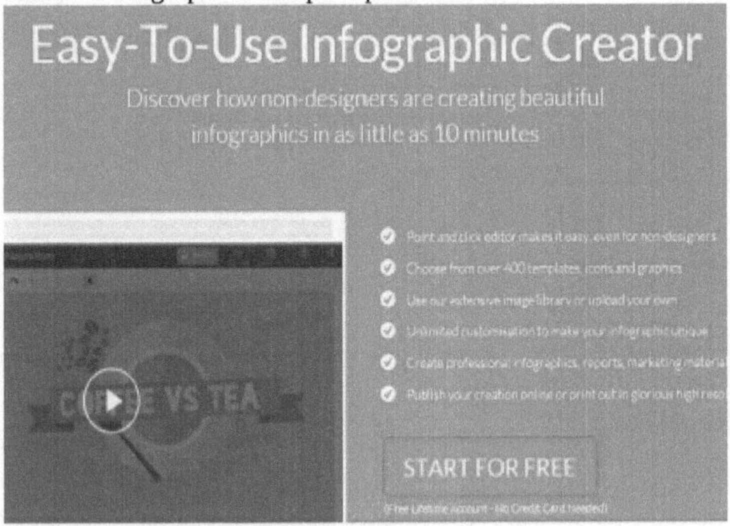

You'll then submit your info graphic on the following websites:
Source: http://www.seerinteractive.com/

http://infographic.co.za/

http://infographicjournal.com/submit-infographics/

http://www.cloudinfographics.com/

http://www.infographicas.com/

http://www.omginfographics.com/

http://www.pureinfographics.com

http://infographipedia.com/

http://infographicsite.com/

http://www.infographiclove.com/

http://videoinfographic.com/submit-infographic/

http://www.infographichub.com/submit-infographics/

http://www.ratemyinfographic.com/post-your-infographic/

http://www.bestinfographics.co.uk/

http://www.infographicgallery.com/

http://www.infographicpost.com/

http://infographr.tumblr.com

http://fuckyeahinfographics.tumblr.com/

http://theinfographics.blogspot.com/

http://infographicsbin.tumblr.com/

http://brandlessblog.com/submit-infographic/

http://www.infographicsking.com/submit-infographic

http://iheartinfographics.tumblr.com/

http://www.info-graphic.co.uk/

http://www.infographicsamples.com/submit-infographic/

http://vizualarchive.com/

http://www.infographicscentral.com/submit-infographic/

http://www.infographicsmaze.com/submit-infographics/

You'll usually get higher ranking results in 2-4 weeks through this method.

AUDIO SHARING SITES

What I like about audio sharing websites is that they are not as highly moderated compared to other sites. Now, that doesn't mean you can just spam the hell out of these websites.

The first thing that you need to do is to record an audio. Just say whatever you want to say about your website. A one minute audio would do.

You can use http://vocaroo.com to record your own voice. Save it as mp3 file.

Now, go to these audio sharing sites and register for a free account.

Simply upload your audios and don't forget to put your website or a backlink to your profile or to the audio you are uploading.

http://bandcamp.com

http://reverbnation.com

http://8tracks.com

http://sutros.com

http://soundcloud.com

http://yourlisten.com

http://mobypicture.com
http://playlist.net
http://wearehunted.com

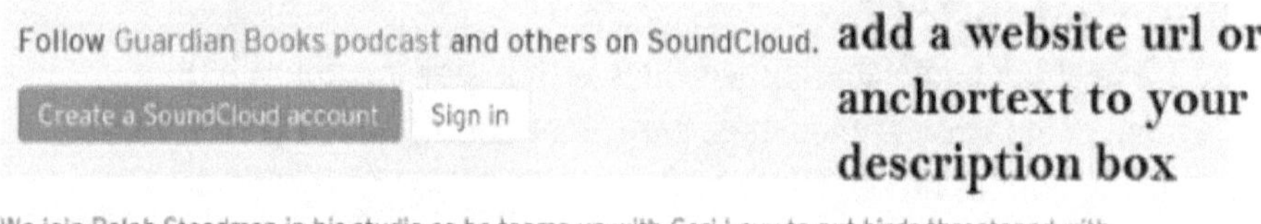

You can also add your own url or anchor text backlink from your audio description box.

With this method, you'll probably get a result in as little as 5 days.

NOTE: REREAD THIS CHAPTER IF IT SEEMS CONFUSING, IT'S REALLY IMPORTANT

Conclusion & Review Request

Thanks for reading this book. This system is not some kind of magic formula that will make you rich overnight, but it is effective and it'll help you make extra cash online. If you like this book and it helped you in some way or another, kindly post a review on Amazon.com. Reviews are the lifeblood of every author out there and it helps in sharing the message.

www.ingramcontent.com/pod-product-compliance
Lightning Source LLC
Chambersburg PA
CBHW031225160726
47992CB00006B/2910